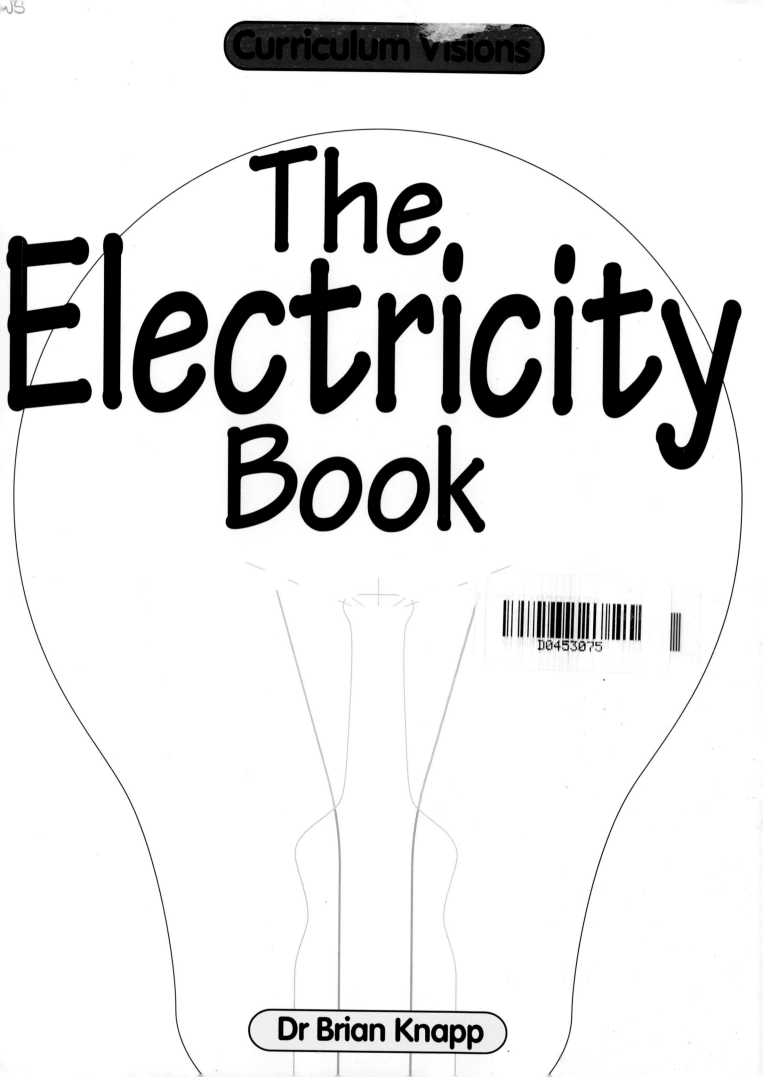

Curriculum Visions

The Electricity Book

Dr Brian Knapp

Atlantic Europe Publishing

First published in 2000 by
Atlantic Europe Publishing Company Ltd

Copyright © 2000
Atlantic Europe Publishing Company Ltd

Author
Brian Knapp, BSc, PhD
Art Director
Duncan McCrae, BSc
Editors
Mary Sanders, BSc and Gillian Gatehouse
Illustrations
David Woodroffe and Nicolas Debon (COVER)
Page make-up
Mark Palmer
Designed and produced by
EARTHSCAPE EDITIONS
Reproduced in Malaysia by
Global Colour
Printed in Hong Kong by
Wing King Tong Company Ltd

Suggested cataloguing location
Knapp, Brian
    The Electricity Book – *Curriculum Visions*
    1. Electricity – Juvenile Literature
        2. Magnetism – Juvenile Literature
    I. Title.
537

ISBN 1 862140 92 8 Hardback
ISBN 1 862140 97 9 Paperback

Picture credits
All photographs are from the Earthscape Editions photolibrary.

This product is manufactured from sustainable managed forests. For every tree cut down at least one more is planted.

Curriculum Visions

Curriculum Visions is a registered trademark of Atlantic Europe Publishing Company Ltd

Glossary
There is a glossary on pages 46–47. Glossary terms are referred to in the text by using CAPITALS like this.

Index
There is an index on page 48.

Teacher's Guide
There is a 'Teacher's Guide' to accompany this book available only from the publisher.

Dedicated Web Site
There is page-by-page support on our dedicated web site. Visit:

www.CurriculumVisions.com

DANGER
Mains electricity can kill. This is why all the interesting things you will find to do in this book use batteries rather than the mains.

Never, never touch exposed mains wires or open anything that is connected to, or is intended to be connected to, the mains. Components inside some mains equipment can give a shock even when not connected to the mains.

The Publisher cannot accept any responsibility for any accidents or injuries that may result from using the information in this book.

Contents

Introduction

Here are some important ideas about electricity and magnetism.

1 **ELECTRICITY** flows through many kinds of materials. Find out which ones on pages 6, 7 and 10.

2 When pieces of electrical equipment are connected together so that electricity flows through them, they form a **CIRCUIT**. See how to make circuits on pages 6, 7 and 12.

3 Electricity is pushed around a circuit by a source of **POWER**. **BATTERIES** are an important portable source of low voltage electricity. Look at how batteries work on page 8.

4 We make use of some materials to conduct electricity and others to insulate us from it. How to find out which they are is shown on page 10.

5 An electric **CURRENT** will flow in a circuit unless the circuit is broken. A switch is one way of breaking a circuit. Find out about **SWITCHES** on page 14.

6 By using switches creatively, you can get circuits to do many useful things. See some examples on pages 16 to 21.

7 When pieces of equipment in a circuit are connected to one another in a single loop, the circuit is called a **SERIES CIRCUIT**. Find out about this on pages 16 and 18.

8 When pieces of equipment are connected side by side, the circuit is called a **PARALLEL CIRCUIT**. See pages 16 and 20.

9 We can find out how electricity flows in wires by using a **CIRCUIT TESTER**. Look at some simple investigations on page 22.

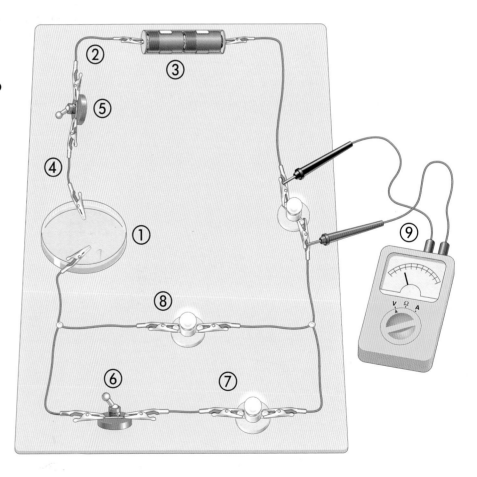

⑩ **MAINS ELECTRICITY** is the most common source of power for artificial lighting. This is shown on page 24.

⑪ Mains electricity is widely used for heating because it is convenient. See this on page 26.

⑫ **FUSES** are used to prevent equipment being damaged by too much power running through them. Fuses are explained on page 28.

⑬ Home electricity is supplied through special home circuits like the one shown on page 30.

⑭ Electricity occurs on the surfaces of many objects. This is called **STATIC ELECTRICITY**. Find out about this on page 32.

⑮ One of the most important results of static electricity is the formation of sparks, including **LIGHTNING**. Find out about this on page 34.

⑯ **MAGNETISM** can be made by metals and by electric currents. See how important this is on page 36.

⑰ **ELECTROMAGNETS** are the main way we use magnetism. This is shown on page 38.

⑱ **ELECTRIC MOTORS** use properties of magnetism and electricity. This is shown on page 40.

⑲ Power supplies convert fuels into electricity. Find out how this works on pages 42 and 44.

⑳ Generation of electricity can have important effects on the environment as shown on page 44.

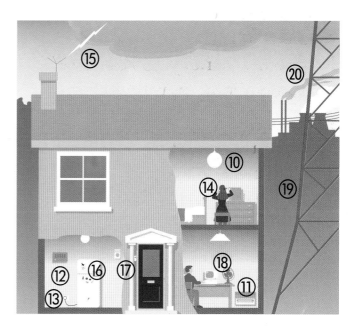

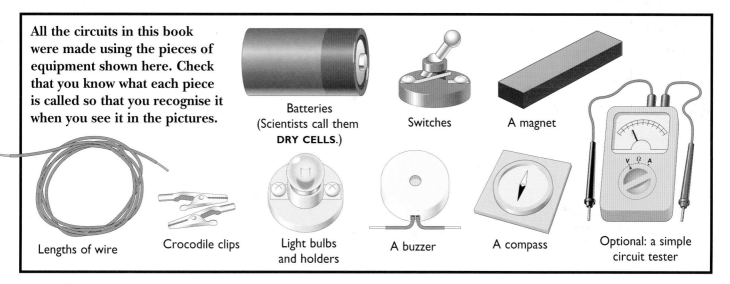

All the circuits in this book were made using the pieces of equipment shown here. Check that you know what each piece is called so that you recognise it when you see it in the pictures.

Batteries (Scientists call them **DRY CELLS**.)

Switches

A magnet

Lengths of wire

Crocodile clips

Light bulbs and holders

A buzzer

A compass

Optional: a simple circuit tester

What electricity can do

An electric current is a flow of electricity. Electricity will flow through many different materials, producing heat, light, sound, movement and magnetism. This makes it one of the most useful forms of energy.

Electricity is a form of ENERGY. We can use it to make things work.

Many materials, but especially metals, allow electricity to flow through them. We call the flow of electricity an ELECTRIC CURRENT (in the same way as a flow of water in a river is a water current).

When electricity flows

In picture ①, opposite, you can see some lengths of wire that join a BATTERY to a LIGHT BULB and a BUZZER and dip into a dish of salty water. One of the connecting wires is also wrapped around a small COMPASS. There is also a SWITCH. All of these things link together and make an ELECTRIC CIRCUIT.

When we close the switch, the bulb immediately lights up and the buzzer sounds. At the same instant, the compass needle 'kicks', swinging around sharply. A few seconds later, the bulb feels warm and, after a few minutes, bubbles form in the salty water.

All these changes have been made because of the flow of electricity.

Many effects

Here is a summary of what electricity does in picture ①:
- flows through solids (the wires)
- flows through liquids (salty water)
- produces light (the bulb)
- produces sound (the buzzer)
- produces heat (the bulb)
- causes a compass needle to turn (causes movement)
- produces MAGNETISM (affects the compass needle)

Always make a loop

Electricity has been able to do all of these things because we have joined up a source of electricity (the battery, a kind of electrical pump) to each of the other items (called COMPONENTS) in a continuous loop, using conducting metal wires.

For anything electrical to work, it has to have at least one continuous loop that includes a source of electrical power, such as a battery.

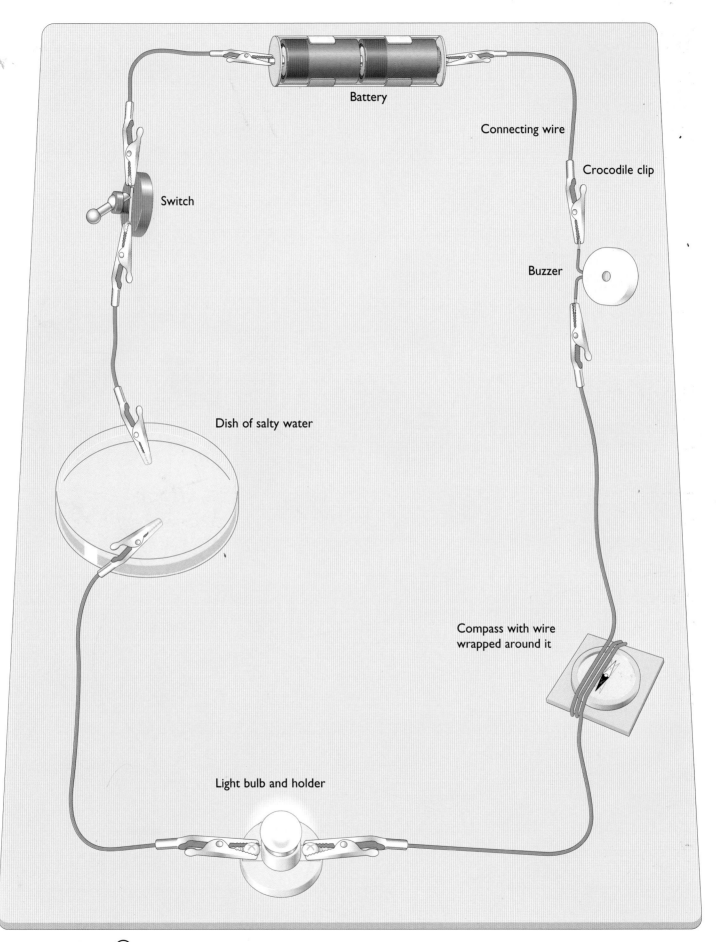

Battery

Connecting wire

Crocodile clip

Switch

Buzzer

Dish of salty water

Compass with wire wrapped around it

Light bulb and holder

▲ ① Heat, light, sound, movement and magnetism can be created using a circuit.

Batteries

For anything electrical to work it has to have a source of electricity. The source of electricity for your circuit is a battery.

A portable supply of electricity is made using a **BATTERY** (also called an 'electric cell' or just a '**CELL**').

What's inside a battery?

A battery does not contain electricity, but instead contains chemicals (pictures ① and ②). It consists of two different materials bathed in a liquid or in a thick paste.

Picture ① shows a side view through a dry battery. You will see that it has a rod of carbon at the centre and a casing of zinc metal. Between them is the thick paste. When the ends of the battery are connected into a circuit, the chemicals react and produce electrical pressure.

All small batteries contain a paste, rather than a liquid, to prevent any chance of leaks and spills. This is why some people call this kind of battery a 'dry battery' (meaning there is no liquid).

Rechargeable batteries

The chemical changes that take place inside a normal dry battery are one-way changes. Once the chemicals have all reacted, the battery will produce no more electricity and can only be disposed of or recycled.

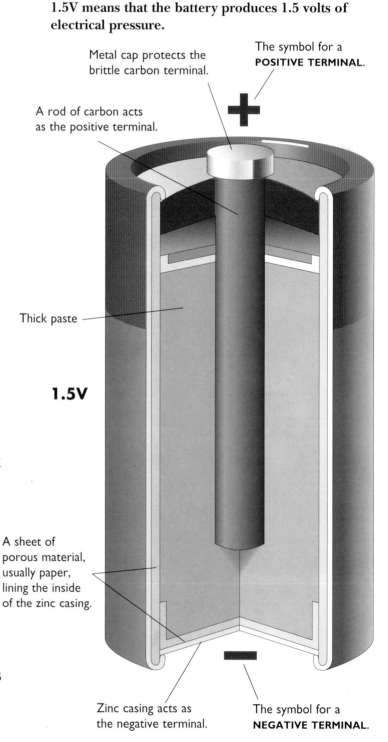

▼ ① **A dry battery. Dry batteries are marked with the 'electrical pressure', or voltage they produce. 1.5V means that the battery produces 1.5 volts of electrical pressure.**

Metal cap protects the brittle carbon terminal.

The symbol for a **POSITIVE TERMINAL**.

A rod of carbon acts as the positive terminal.

Thick paste

1.5V

A sheet of porous material, usually paper, lining the inside of the zinc casing.

Zinc casing acts as the negative terminal.

The symbol for a **NEGATIVE TERMINAL**.

▼ ② This is a car battery. In this case the materials used are lead (which is why car batteries are heavy) and the liquid is sulphuric acid. This combination produces 2 volts of electricity. A car battery is made of six 2V units connected end to end to make 12V.

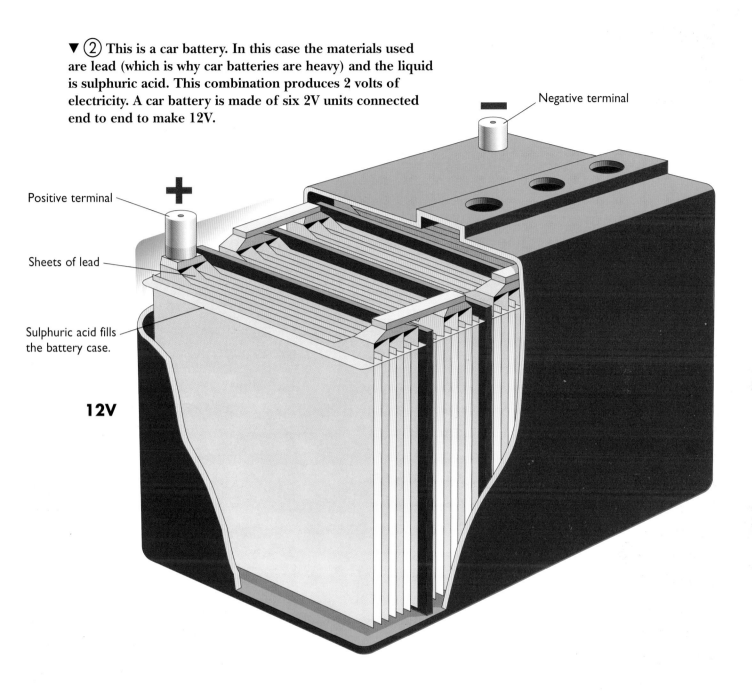

Negative terminal

Positive terminal

Sheets of lead

Sulphuric acid fills the battery case.

12V

Some batteries are rechargeable, however. A car battery, which contains a liquid (picture ②) and some types of more expensive dry battery, can be recharged by passing electricity through them from time to time. This reverses the chemical changes and charges up the battery again.

Rechargeable dry batteries cannot produce as much power as non-rechargeable dry batteries of the same size.

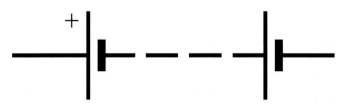

+

▲ This is the symbol for a battery.

Conductors and insulators

Electricity can only flow through some materials. These are called conductors.

We may take it for granted that electricity flows in a wire. But why doesn't it spill out of the wire and flow through the air, for example?

The answer is that electricity can only travel through certain substances. These are called **ELECTRICAL CONDUCTORS**.

Conductors

Metals are the most commonly used conductors. Most of the wires you will use to make circuits contain many thin strands of copper twisted together (picture ①).

Many liquids are also conductors. Salty water or the water in our taps and rivers (which has minerals dissolved in it) is a conductor (see page 6). As a result, touching electrical things with wet hands can make you part of an electrical circuit – and this can be dangerous.

Insulators

Materials that do not let electricity pass through them are called **ELECTRICAL INSULATORS**. Plastics are examples of insulators. They are used, for example, as a sleeve around wires (picture ①), on switches (see page 14) and as plug cases (see page 29).

▼ ① These three wires all contain twisted strands of copper which is a good conductor. The coloured sleeves are made of plastic because it is a good insulator.

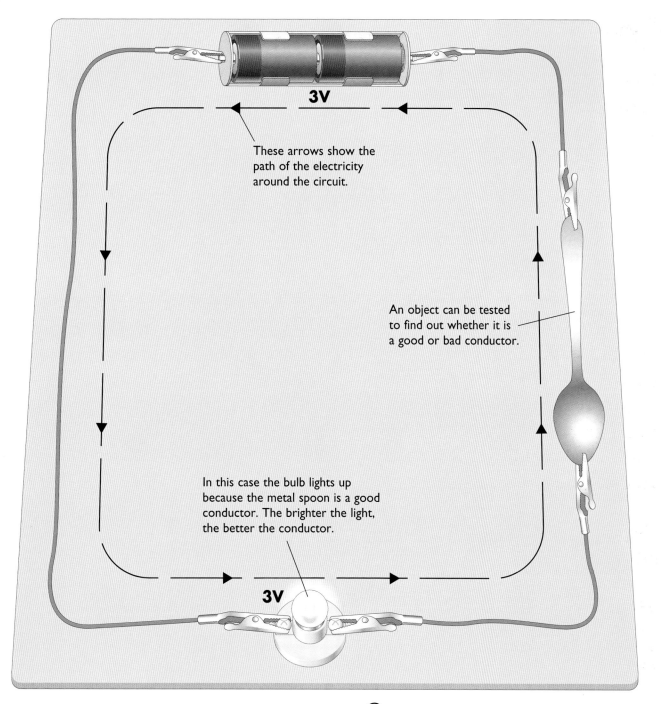

These arrows show the path of the electricity around the circuit.

An object can be tested to find out whether it is a good or bad conductor.

In this case the bulb lights up because the metal spoon is a good conductor. The brighter the light, the better the conductor.

3V

3V

▲ ② In this picture a metal spoon is being tested. The bulb lights up, proving that the metal of the spoon is a conductor.

Air is a good insulator. This is why electricity does not spark down from the pylons that carry power around the country (see page 43).

Conductor or insulator?

One way to find out which materials are insulators and which are conductors is to make a loop (electrical circuit) using a battery and a bulb (picture ②). If the object being tested is a conductor, the electricity will flow through the whole circuit and the bulb will light up. If the object is an insulator, the electricity cannot flow around the circuit and the bulb will not light up.

Circuit diagrams

Circuit diagrams are a way of showing what is happening in a circuit. They are like an electrician's route map.

A **CIRCUIT** is a <u>continuous</u> path for a flow of electricity.

To make a circuit, one end of a battery must be connected by wires to **COMPONENTS** such as bulbs, which in turn are connected back to the <u>other</u> end of the battery.

The simplest kind of circuit connects just two things. Picture ①

shows a simple circuit with a battery connected to a light bulb.

A circuit diagram

It is useful to be able to draw a diagram of how the wires, the battery and the lamp are connected up.

▼ ① **This is an electrical circuit connecting a battery to a light bulb by two wires.**

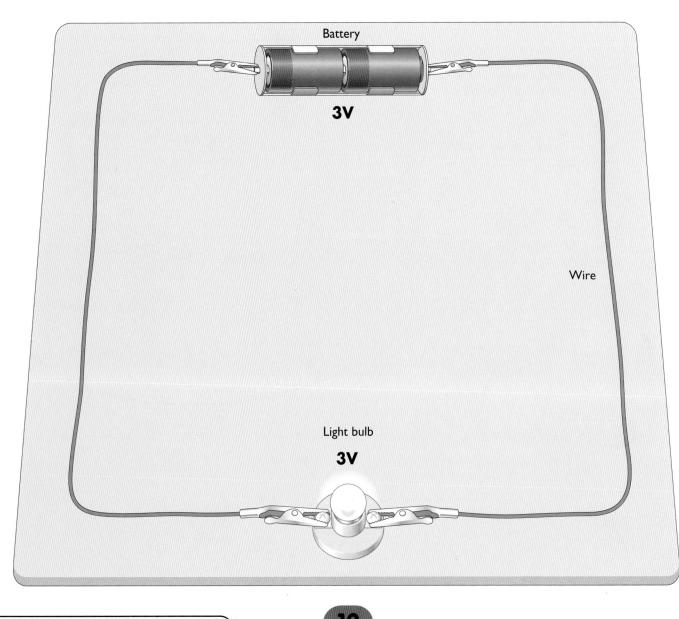

Battery

3V

Wire

Light bulb

3V

Because not all batteries and light bulbs look the same, the diagram will be easier to draw if we use simple symbols in much the same way as map-makers use symbols for roads, rivers, towns and so on.

This line is a symbol for a wire:

This is a symbol for a light bulb:

This is a symbol for a battery:

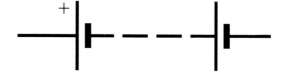

A battery has two connectors, called terminals. The **POSITIVE TERMINAL** is marked with a + sign.

Picture ② shows how these symbols are used to make a circuit diagram that matches the circuit shown in picture ①.

Notice, in this diagram, that the wires are drawn as straight lines with right angle bends.

▼ ② This is a CIRCUIT DIAGRAM. It shows each of the components of picture ① as symbols.

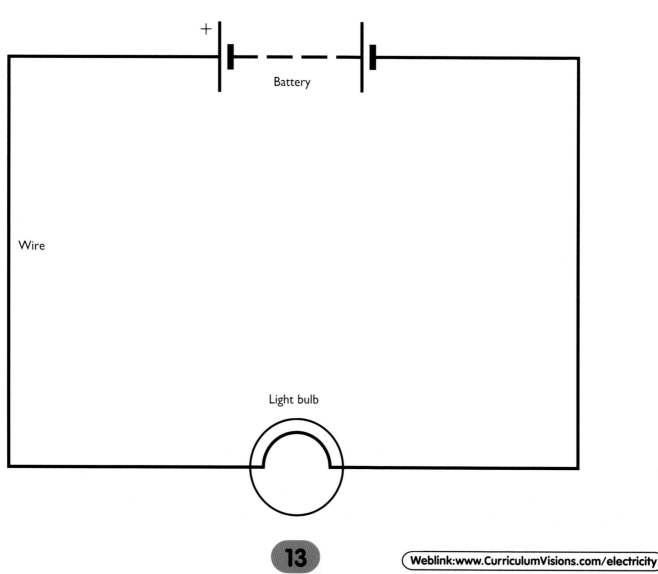

Battery

Wire

Light bulb

Switches: breaking the circuit

Switches are used to break the circuit and control the flow of electricity.

An electric current flows when all of the parts of a circuit make at least one loop. Electricity flows from one end, or terminal, of the battery, through the wires, bulbs, and whatever else is connected, and then back to the other end, or terminal, of the battery.

The current flows because every part is joined. If one part of the circuit is not joined to the next, no current flows and the circuit does not work.

This is not always a bad thing. For example, we may not want to leave the light bulb on all the time until the battery is worn out.

The switch

To stop the flow of electricity, we could simply pull the wires off the bulb or the battery, but this is slow and awkward and the wires would soon get broken.

A **SWITCH** is a small device that reliably breaks and remakes the circuit. The switch in picture ① contains two springy metal plates called **CONTACTS**. When the switch is turned off (opened), the contacts spring apart.

You can see how a switch works in pictures ② and ③. When the switch

is turned on (closed), the contacts are pushed together (picture ③) and the bulb lights up; when the switch is off, the contacts spring apart and the bulb goes off (picture ②).

Notice that, although the contacts move inside the switch and the light comes on and off, the symbols for a switch and a light bulb never change. The symbols show just the components of the circuit and not what is happening in the circuit.

▼ ① **A switch and its symbol look like this.**

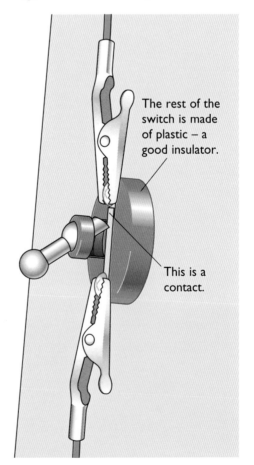

The rest of the switch is made of plastic – a good insulator.

This is a contact.

▶ ② The circuit with a switch in it looks like this. Here the switch is off.

Notice that the contacts are separated when the switch is 'off' or 'open'.

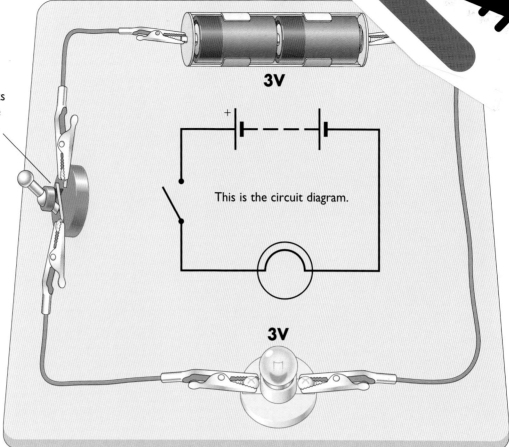

3V

This is the circuit diagram.

3V

▶ ③ Now the switch is at the 'on' position. Notice the contacts are closed. Notice also that the symbol for the switch on the circuit diagram does not change. This is because the circuit just shows you how the components are linked up, <u>not</u> what they do.

Notice that the contacts are pushed together when the switch is 'on' or 'closed'.

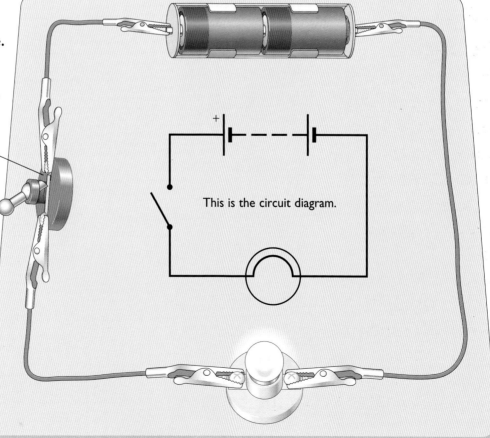

This is the circuit diagram.

Weblink:www.CurriculumVisions.com/electricity

Using two switches

Switches can be used in some clever ways to make circuits do all kinds of things.

Switches can be used rather like the points in a train shunting yard. By clever use of switches, some components can be disconnected from the circuit or switched back on again.

Switches in a circuit with one loop

In picture ① there is a battery, a bulb and two switches. (This is called a **SERIES CIRCUIT**; see also page 18.)

If only one of the switches is closed (on), the bulb will not light

▼ ① **A circuit with two switches.**

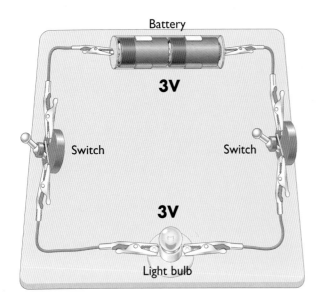

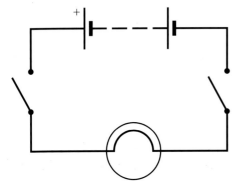

up. This is because the circuit is still broken at the other switch. Both switches have to be closed for the bulb to light up.

A circuit with two loops

The circuit diagram in picture ② shows a circuit with a battery, two switches and two bulbs. (This is called a **PARALLEL CIRCUIT**; see page 20.) Follow it around carefully, starting from the positive terminal of the battery, to see what happens.

A wire leaves the positive terminal of the battery going left across the top of the circuit. Notice that it arrives at a junction – a place where wires are joined together. The symbol for a junction on the circuit diagram is a 'blob':

From this junction there are now two routes for electricity to follow. Route A goes straight down, then through a switch and a bulb to another junction.

Route B goes down to another switch and then to another bulb.

Note: a computer processor is simply millions of tiny switches arranged in a complicated way. You can't get a more clever use of switches than that!

▼ ② A circuit with two switches in parallel.

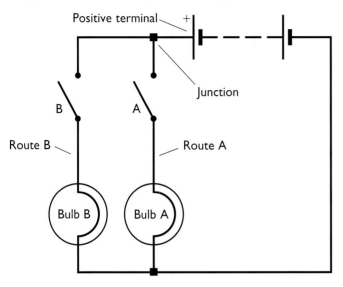

Positive terminal   +

Junction

B   A

Route B   Route A

Bulb B   Bulb A

▼ ③ The four possible combinations that can be achieved with two switches and two light bulbs using a parallel circuit.

Both routes meet again at a junction at the bottom of the diagram and then go directly to the negative terminal of the battery to complete the circuit.

This is a clever circuit, because we can now have the left-hand bulb switched on with the right-hand bulb switched off, or the left-hand one on and the right-hand one off, or both on together, or both off together. Four combinations of lights are possible from two switches (picture ③)!

This is the principle on which the lights in your home or school work.

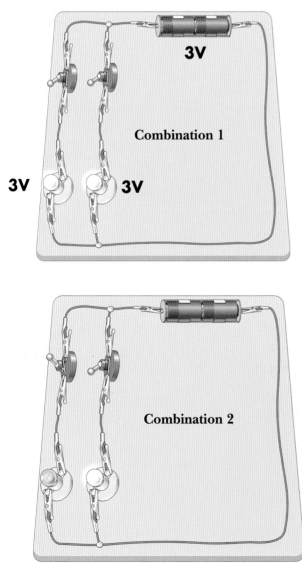

3V

Combination 1

3V   3V

Combination 2

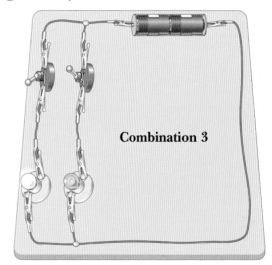

Combination 3

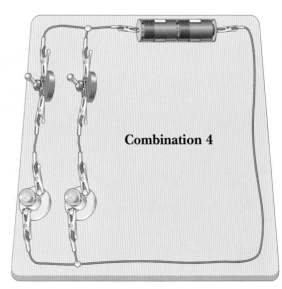

Combination 4

Weblink:www.CurriculumVisions.com/electricity

Series circuits

When all of the electrical equipment is connected in a ring, it is called a series circuit.

There are two ways you can connect up electrical equipment. You can string it all together in a single loop. When this happens you are making a **SERIES CIRCUIT** (picture ①). An alternative **PARALLEL CIRCUIT** is shown on page 20.

Most (but not all) of the circuits we have looked at on the previous pages have been connected together in a single series loop.

Looking at a series circuit

Picture ① shows a battery connected in a loop to a switch and two light bulbs. Picture ② shows this as a circuit diagram. Notice that each of the light bulbs forms part of a single

loop; <u>there are no junctions</u>. This proves it is a series circuit.

If you were to make this circuit and switch it on, you would find the bulbs shine with a dimmer light than when the circuit has just one bulb.

To make the light bulbs shine more brightly there have to be more batteries. This shows that, the more bulbs (or any other components) you

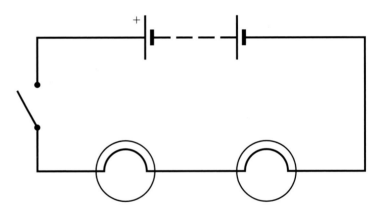

▼ ① This is a series circuit with 2 bulbs in a continuous loop.

▲ ② The circuit diagram for picture ①.

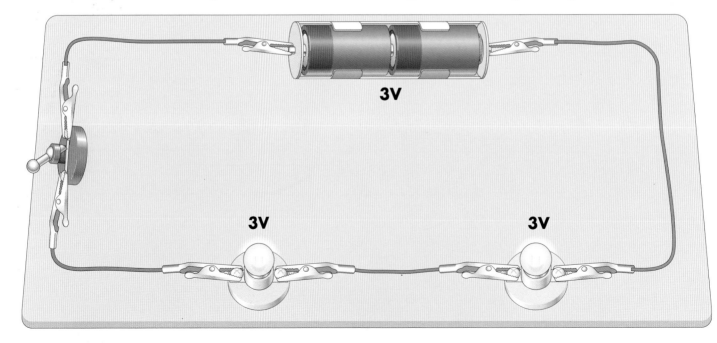

3V

3V   3V

have strung together in a line (in series), the more batteries are needed to keep the items working at full strength.

Matching the battery to the light bulbs

Batteries are labelled in volts. You will see the number of volts written down the side of the battery. A normal rod-shaped dry battery produces 1.5 volts of electricity. Bulbs are also labelled in volts. The number is written on the metal base.

To get a bright light, make sure that the sum of all the numbers on the bulbs is the same as the sum of all the numbers on the batteries. Some results of increasing the number of batteries are shown in pictures ③ and ④. The circuit is shown in picture ⑤.

As you can see, when there are lots of items in a series circuit, lots of batteries are needed. You can find out how to get over this problem on page 20.

▶ ③ A series circuit with dimly shining light bulbs. In this case there are three 3V bulbs but only two 1.5V batteries. The sum of the bulbs (3 + 3 + 3 = 9) does not match the sum of the batteries (1.5 + 1.5 = 3) and so the bulbs will be very dim.

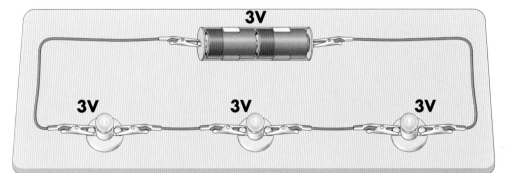

▶ ④ A series circuit with six batteries (1.5 + 1.5 + 1.5 + 1.5 + 1.5 + 1.5 = 9) and three 3V bulbs (3 + 3 + 3 = 9). The sum of the voltages match, and so the bulbs will shine brightly.

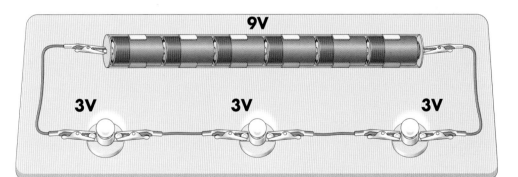

▶ ⑤ The circuit diagram for 3 bulbs in series.

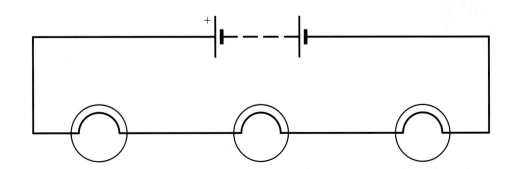

Parallel circuits

In parallel circuits, each item shares a direct connection to a battery.

We can connect components such as light bulbs so that each one is attached directly to the battery. When we do this, we say the items in the circuit are connected in parallel (pictures ① and ②). Notice that there are four junctions. The presence of junctions proves it is parallel wiring.

Picture ① shows three light bulbs connected to a battery in a **PARALLEL CIRCUIT**.

Picture ② shows this parallel circuit as a circuit diagram.

The advantages of parallel wiring

When items are connected in parallel, no matter how many items you connect up, every one will work just as well as when there is only one item

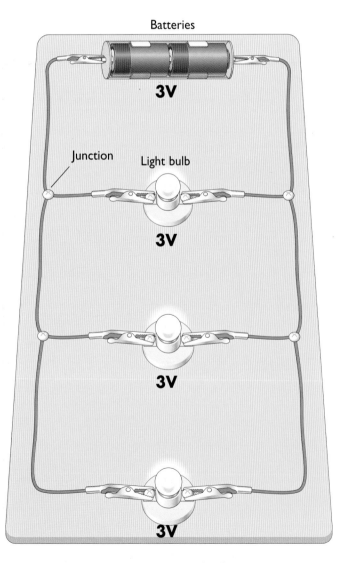

▲ ① A parallel circuit using light bulbs.

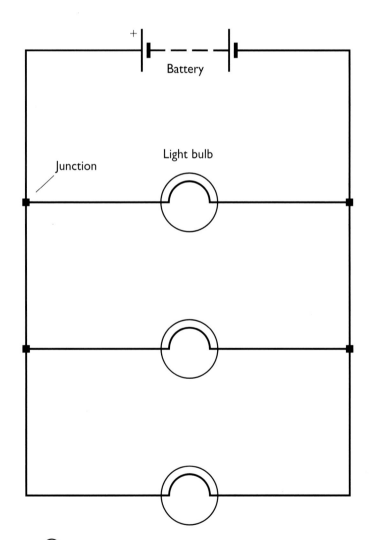

▲ ② A circuit diagram of a parallel circuit using light bulbs.

connected. (However, the more items you connect, the more power is needed to run them and the faster the battery will run out!)

You can prove that it makes no difference how many light bulbs you use with the circuit in picture ③, which uses switches. Picture ④ shows the circuit diagram.

Look carefully at the circuit and notice that the top bulb will always shine because two wires connect it directly to the battery.

The middle bulb will light if the middle switch is closed (on) and the bottom bulb will light if the bottom switch is closed (on). When each bulb lights, it will be as bright as the others, whether three, two or just one bulb is on.

Uses for parallel circuits

The electricity supply in your home, school and in most buildings is an example of parallel wiring. This means that you can connect as many items as you need to the electricity supply.

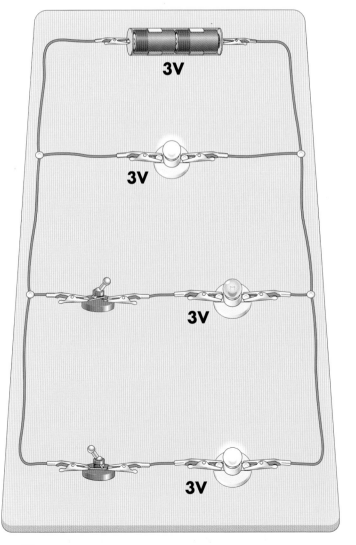

▲ ③ A parallel circuit using light bulbs and switches.

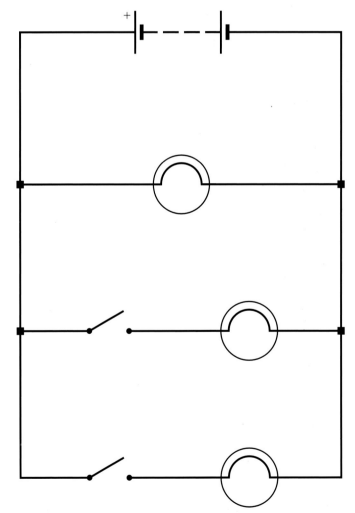

▲ ④ A circuit diagram of a parallel circuit using light bulbs and switches.

Weblink:www.CurriculumVisions.com/electricity

Circuit testing

You cannot always see what is happening inside a circuit, so a special piece of equipment, called a circuit tester, is designed to help you.

A **CIRCUIT TESTER** is a simple, easy-to-use, measuring device for finding out what is happening in an electric circuit, just as a stethoscope helps a doctor find out what is going on inside a body (picture ①).

Three simple measurements are shown here.

Investigating a battery

A battery provides the 'pressure' that makes the current flow through the circuit. The amount of 'pressure' is called the **VOLTAGE**. A normal dry battery produces 1.5 volts of electric 'pressure'.

To use a circuit tester to find out the voltage, set the circuit tester to read 'V', for volts. To find the voltage of a battery, for example, put the red (positive) lead from the circuit tester on to the positive battery terminal, and the other lead on to the other terminal (picture ②). The needle will

▲ ① This is a circuit tester, also called a meter or multimeter. Two leads (called probes) allow it to be attached to any part of a circuit.

Most circuit testers can do three things: measure the electric current (when set to A, for amps); measure voltage (when set to V for volts); and measure how good a conductor something is (when set to Ω for ohms).

▼ ② If a circuit does not work, always test the batteries to make sure they are not worn out.

This is how you test a battery. The circuit tester is set to V, for volts. A 1.5V battery should read 1.5 on the circuit tester scale. If it reads 1.3 or 1.2, it is nearly worn out. If it reads nothing at all, it is completely used up. If the needle tries to turn to the left, you have the leads connected the wrong way round; just reverse the leads and the needle will swing to the right.

move and you can read the voltage from the scale on the circuit tester.

Investigating a broken circuit

You can use a circuit tester to find out if there is a break in your circuit. You can use the circuit tester in this way to find out if a wire, a light bulb or a

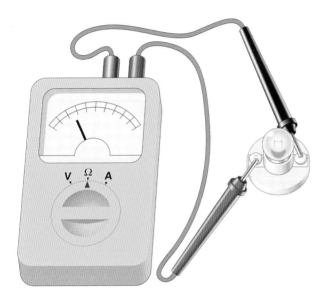

▲ ③ This is how you test a light bulb. First, make sure the bulb is screwed tightly into its holder. The circuit tester is then set to Ω, for ohms. The needle should swing right across the scale. If it reads nothing at all then the bulb filament is broken and the bulb needs to be replaced.

fuse is broken. The circuit tester has to be set to 'Ω', which is the symbol for **OHMS**. Place one lead on each side of the item under test (picture ③). If the needle swings, the item is not broken.

Measuring current

The flow of electricity is called the **ELECTRIC CURRENT**. To read the electric current, the circuit tester dial is set to 'A' for **AMPS**, the measurement of electric current.

To read the current, the circuit tester is placed inside the loop of the circuit (picture ④).

If you were to put the circuit tester in a different place in the circuit, for example, between two other bulbs, you would find that the current reading was just the same. This tells us that, in a series circuit, the same current flows through every part of the circuit.

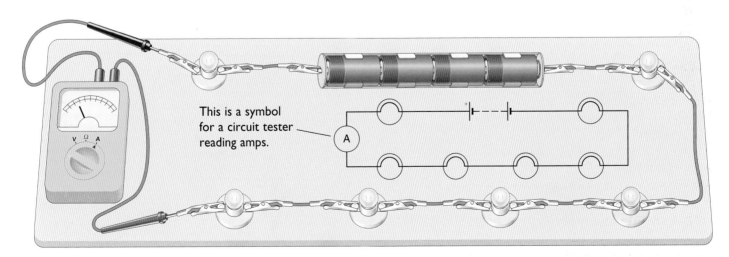

This is a symbol for a circuit tester reading amps.

▲ ④ An electric current flows through every part of the circuit. The <u>same</u> amount of current flows through every part of the circuit.

Using mains electricity for light

Most of the electricity we use is mains electricity. This is because we need more power than batteries can provide.

Filament lamps

When a wire carries a large current compared with its size, it gives out light. The wire, or **FILAMENT**, in a **LIGHT BULB** (picture ①) is designed to give out as much light as possible. The filament is made into a long, tight coil, so that it can give out as much light as needed while staying in a compact shape.

Bulbs can be made to give out different amounts of light. The more light a bulb gives out, the more **POWER** is needed to make it work. So bulbs marked as 100W (W = watts) give out four times as much light as 25W bulbs but also use four times as much power.

As the current flows through the thin filament, it glows 'white hot' (picture ②). It is not possible for a filament to give out light without giving out heat as well. In fact, only about a tenth of the electrical energy

▼ ① **The parts of a light bulb.**

Glass bulb

Inert gas inside bulb

▲▼ Filament heats up when light is switched on.

▼ ② **The brighter (whiter) the light, the more efficient the bulb.**

Wires run from the connections to the filament.

Cap has either a bayonet (front) or screw fitting (behind) to hold the bulb in the socket so that the connections are in contact with the mains supply.

Connections to lamp

put through a light bulb is used in making light, the other nine-tenths is 'wasted' as heat. This 'wasted heat' is the reason why ordinary light bulbs become very hot when in use.

Halogen lamps

The halogen lamp was invented in the 1950s. It is made of a wire filament inside a very small bulb filled with a special 'halogen' gas (picture ③). The special gas allows the filament to burn hotter and, therefore, give out a whiter light than ordinary filament lamps. It also uses less energy, lasts much longer, and does not grow dim with use.

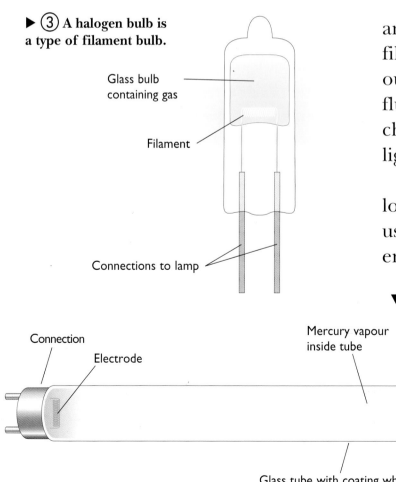

▶ ③ A halogen bulb is a type of filament bulb.

Glass bulb containing gas

Filament

Connections to lamp

Fluorescent lamps

A fluorescent lamp is another way of converting electrical energy into light (picture ④).

A fluorescent lamp does not have a filament. The gas inside the tube is mercury vapour. When the power supply is connected, the mercury vapour conducts the electricity. This causes the mercury vapour to give off an invisible light called ultraviolet light.

The inside surface of the fluorescent tube is coated with a material that will give out white light when it is struck by ultraviolet light. This is called fluorescence.

Although it is more complicated and more expensive to make than a filament bulb, very little heat is given out in this kind of lamp. This is why a fluorescent tube is more efficient and cheaper to operate than a filament light bulb.

A fluorescent tube lasts ten times longer than a filament light bulb, and uses about a fifth of the electrical energy for the same amount of light.

▼ ④ An fluorescent lamp in the shape of a tube.

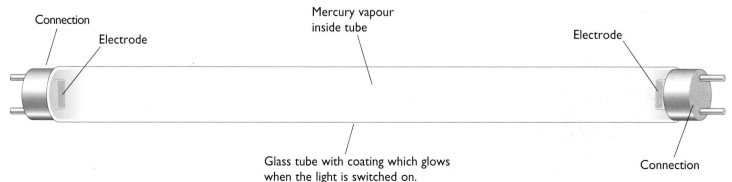

Connection

Electrode

Mercury vapour inside tube

Electrode

Glass tube with coating which glows when the light is switched on.

Connection

Using mains electricity for heat

When a large current flows through a thin wire, it will get hot. This is how a heating element works.

When electricity flows through a wire, some of the electricity is changed into heat.

Heating elements

There are occasions when it is very useful to have wires that heat up in a controlled way, such as when we use electricity for heating.

If you look at an electric fire (picture ①) you will see that the heating part – called the heating element – is made of a coil of wire. This is special wire that does not melt when it becomes red hot.

When the heater is switched on the current flows through the heating element just as it would flow through a lamp. So, the circuit diagram is really very simple (picture ②).

Remember that when a wire carries a large current compared with

▼ ② **This is a circuit diagram of an electric fire.**

Mains

Switch

Heating element

We use this saw-tooth symbol for any object that slows down, or resists, the flow of electricity.

▼ ① **This is a single-bar electric fire.**

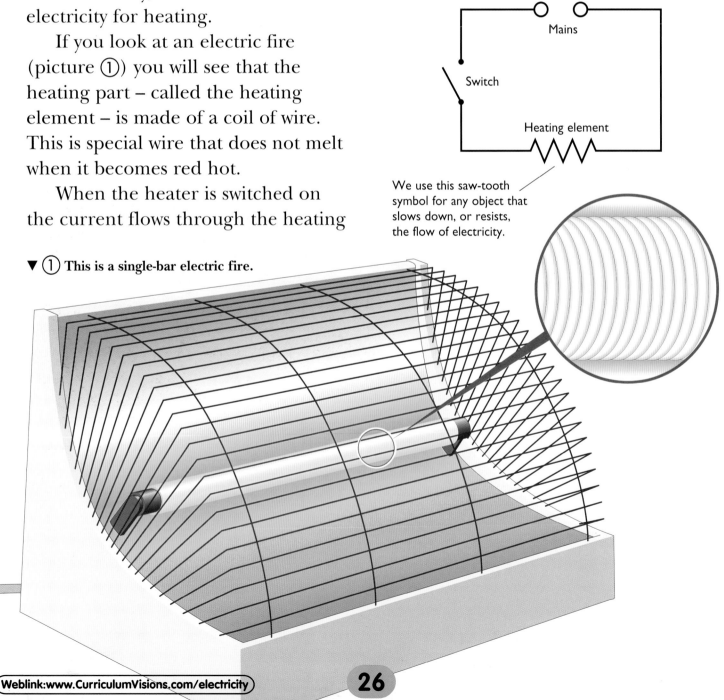

its size, it can give out both heat and light. A heater needs to give out as much heat as possible and light is not wanted. The wires are, therefore, made thicker than in a light bulb. The dull orange glow you see in an electric fire is unwanted light.

▲ ③ This shows the heating element in a kettle.

▼ ④ This shows the heating element in an iron.

Appliances that use heating elements

Heating elements look very different, depending on where they are needed, but the circuit is always the same.

Here are common places where heating elements are found:

- toasters
- electric kettles (picture ③)
- electric blankets
- electric heaters or fires (picture ①)
- electric water heaters
- electric showers
- electric irons (picture ④)
- electric ovens, grills and hot plates (picture ⑤).

▲ ⑤ This is an element from a cooker. Because you need to stand heavy pans on a cooker, the heating wire is inside a strong metal tube. The wire is also insulated from the tube so that there is no chance of an electric shock.

Fuses

A fuse is an emergency switch. It is a thin wire which will easily melt and break the flow of electricity when a circuit becomes overloaded.

Imagine a circuit wire as being like a pipe full of water. The wider the pipe, the more water it can carry. Normally, electrical currents flow quite slowly through the wires of a circuit, just as water might flow slowly through a big pipe.

What happens when you try to force a lot of electricity around a circuit? The answer is that the electrical flow speeds up (picture ①). Just as fast-moving water brushes against the walls of the pipe and warms it up. So, fast-moving electricity makes a wire get warm.

Fuses

It is often dangerous to allow wires to heat up because they may be touching materials that could catch fire. But there is one place where wires are made especially thin, and this is in a safety device called a **FUSE**.

A fuse is a small length of thin wire made of a metal that melts easily as it heats up (picture ②). When the wire melts, the circuit is broken. When this happens, people say that the 'fuse has blown'.

Fuse wire is kept in special safety holders to prevent the melting wire from touching anything that could catch fire.

▼ ① A fuse is a very thin wire with a low melting point. The value of the fuse is matched to the circuit to make sure it is the first thing to fail.

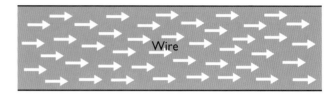

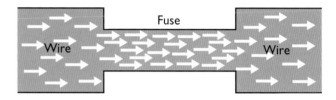

▼ ② The stages of a fuse blowing.

No overload. Fuse wire is cool.

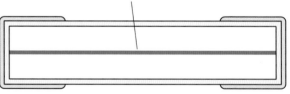

Overload beginning. Fuse wire heats up and expands.

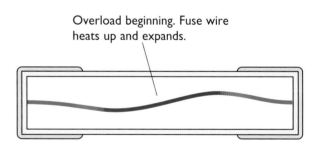

Fuse wire melts safely inside tube and circuit is broken.

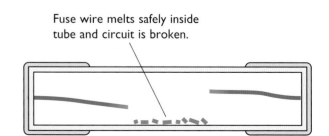

Fuses and circuits

Fuses are important in most electrical circuits. Without a fuse, some other part of the wiring could heat up, perhaps a part hidden inside a wall of a house, or under the floor, or in a motor car. This could cause a fire.

If you have a thick fuse wire in a circuit where the other wires are thin, the fuse wire may not be the first to melt and so the whole purpose of the fuse would be lost. But if the fuse wire is too thin in a circuit, it will keep melting and the **APPLIANCES** will never work. Fuses must be matched to the circuits they are used in.

Appliances are always separately fused. If they were not, the appliance might be damaged and catch fire before the fuse melts in the home

circuit. Pictures ③ and ④ show typical fuses and where they are found.

Fuses that are fitted inside plugs are always labelled to show what their values are. Lights, radios, TVs and the like are protected by either a 3A or a 5A fuse, while kettles and similar appliances are protected by a 13A fuse. A 13A fuse must <u>never</u> be used in a circuit for low-power electrical equipment.

This is a symbol for a fuse:

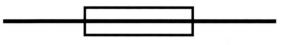

▶ ④ **This is a fuse inside a plug. The cover of the plug has been removed so that you can see it clearly. The fuse is in the 'live' part of the circuit.**

▼ ③ **A 13 amp and a 5 amp fuse.**

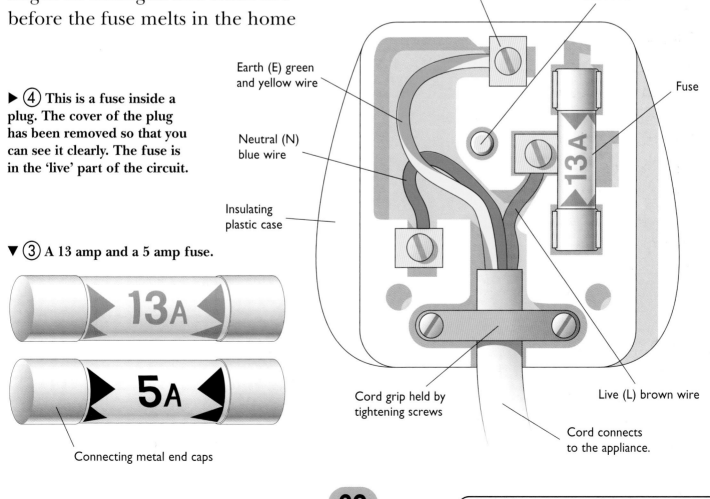

Screw connectors hold wires in place.

Screw to attach lid

Fuse

Earth (E) green and yellow wire

Neutral (N) blue wire

Insulating plastic case

13A

5A

Connecting metal end caps

Cord grip held by tightening screws

Live (L) brown wire

Cord connects to the appliance.

Home circuits

Your home electricity supply makes use of the circuits and fuses shown on the previous pages.

The design of home supply circuits uses many of the ideas you have seen in the earlier parts of this book. In particular you need to remember about parallel circuits (page 20), power and fuses (page 28), the power used by big appliances such as heaters (page 26), and the power used by light bulbs (page 24). In picture ① you see all of this information put to good, safe use.

Follow the electric current of the mains as it enters from the street.

Supply

The electricity supply company connects your home to the cable in the street through a fuse (**A**). This is to prevent an electrical problem in your home from causing problems to other homes in the neighbourhood, or for problems from any other home affecting yours.

Meter

The meter (**B**) records the amount of electrical energy you use in your home every second. You can see how much you are using by watching the numbers change on the meter.

Fuse box

The supply from the meter goes to a main switch (**C**) and fuse box (**D**)

inside your home. If you turn this switch off, all the power to your house will be cut. It's important to have this switch in case of an emergency or in case an electrician wants to alter the house wiring or to replace a fuse.

Notice that small 5A fuses (**E**) protect the lighting circuit, and larger 15A fuses protect the wall sockets (**F**). Appliances that use very large amounts of electricity (such as immersion heaters, storage heaters and cookers) each have their own supply (**G**).

Ring circuits

Two cables go to every item that needs electricity (**H**). The LIVE WIRE (brown) brings electricity to the appliances, the NEUTRAL WIRE (blue) carries it away. The green wire used in some circuits (**J**) is an EARTH WIRE. This is a protection device to carry electricity safely away if a fault develops.

The circuit for the sockets and circuit for the lights are both examples of parallel circuits.

All of the light fittings and the sockets use built-in switches.

Live ⎯⎯⎯⎯⎯⎯⎯⎯

Neutral ⎯⎯⎯⎯⎯⎯⎯⎯

Earth ⎯⎯⎯⎯⎯⎯⎯⎯

▼ ① This wiring diagram shows the parallel circuits used to feed electricity through a home.

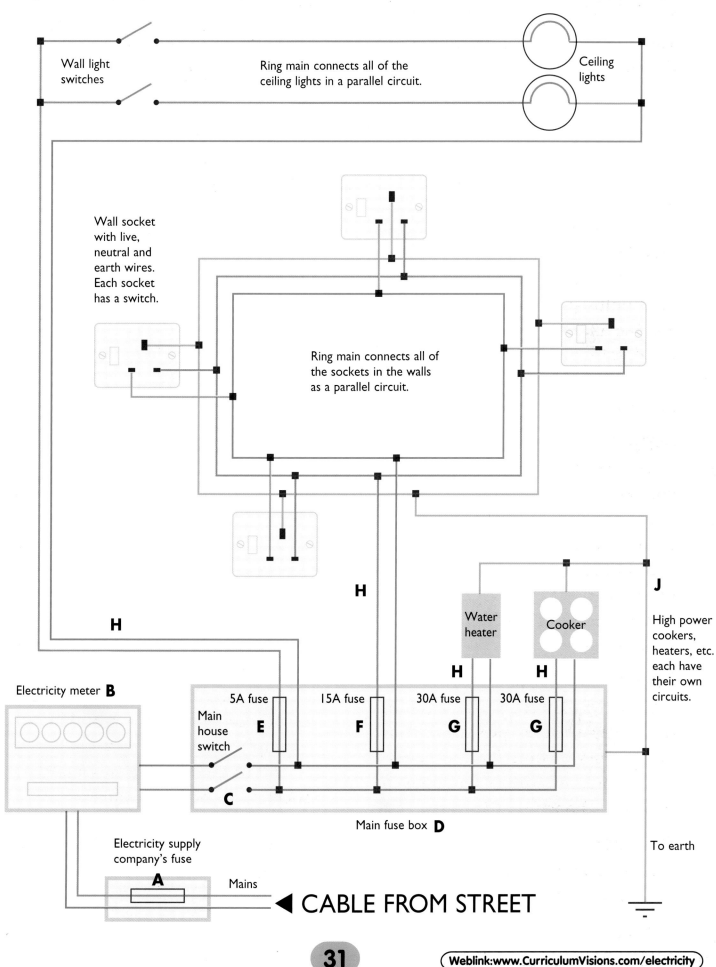

Wall light switches

Ring main connects all of the ceiling lights in a parallel circuit.

Ceiling lights

Wall socket with live, neutral and earth wires. Each socket has a switch.

Ring main connects all of the sockets in the walls as a parallel circuit.

H

H

H

Water heater

Cooker

H

H

J

High power cookers, heaters, etc. each have their own circuits.

Electricity meter **B**

5A fuse

15A fuse

30A fuse

30A fuse

Main house switch

E

F

G

G

C

Main fuse box **D**

Electricity supply company's fuse

A

Mains

To earth

◀ CABLE FROM STREET

Surface electricity

Electricity forms on the surface of many objects. It is called static electricity.

All of the electricity we have dealt with so far flows inside conductors. But electricity also forms on the surfaces of insulators. This kind of electricity cannot move about and so it is called **STATIC ELECTRICITY** (the word static means 'not moving'). Static electricity flows away (it is discharged) if the surface is touched by a conductor.

How static electricity is formed

Static electricity has to be made, or generated. Static electricity is produced when insulators rub together (pictures ① and ②).

Static electricity is removed by touching a metal object because then the electricity will be conducted away.

Opposites attract

You may have noticed that electricity has opposites. In electricity the opposites are called positive and negative. A battery, for example, has a positive end and a negative end (see page 8). Electricity flows in a circuit because positive and negatives attract. In static electricity we use the words positive **CHARGE** and negative charge for the build-up of electricity on the surface.

▼▶ ① **How charges form on the surface of materials. Before rubbing (left) and after rubbing (right).**

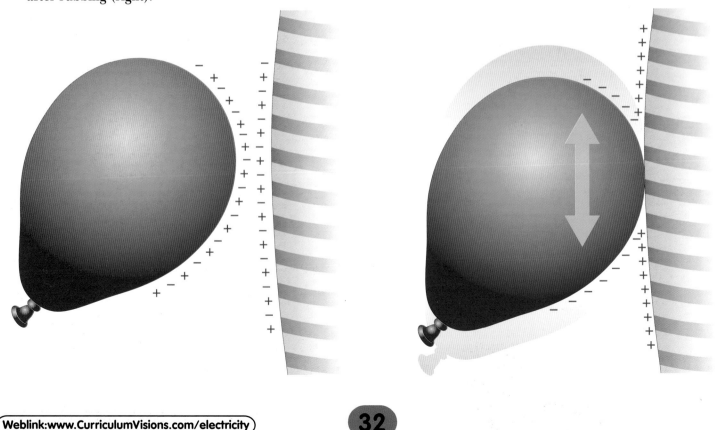

The surface of all insulators have positive and negative charges on them, but they are usually in balance and so they are not noticeable.

When materials rub together, positive charges are rubbed off from one surface and on to the other. As a result, one surface has more negative charges than normal and the other surface has more positive charges (picture ①).

Positive charges attract negative charges. You can see this when a balloon is placed near a jumper after the two have been rubbed together. The balloon holds fast to the jumper as though it were stuck there (picture ②). This is the result of all

▲ ③ This is a special piece of equipment that generates static electricity. By touching the machine, the static electricity is transferred from the machine to the tips of the hair.

▼ ② After rubbing the balloons on the jumper they appear to stick, as if by magic. This is static electricity.

the positive charges on one material attracting the negative charges on the other material.

After a while the negative and positive charges will recombine and the balloon will fall off.

Like charges repel

Whereas opposite charges attract, like charges repel.

Picture ③ shows a girl with her hair standing on end! She is touching a machine which generates static electricity. The electricity has gone across the surface of her body and into her hair. But the charges that reach the ends of her hair are all the same. Because like charges repel, the hairs try to get as far away from each other as possible, which makes them stand on end.

Weblink:www.CurriculumVisions.com/electricity

Sparks and lightning

Electricity can jump between two surfaces when the difference in electric charge is great. The jump is seen as a spark. Lightning is the world's largest spark.

One of the most curious effects in nature is a **SPARK**. The world's biggest sparks are called **LIGHTNING**, but there are many other natural sparks, as well.

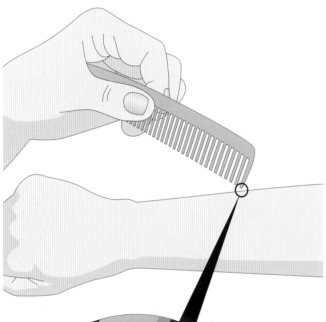

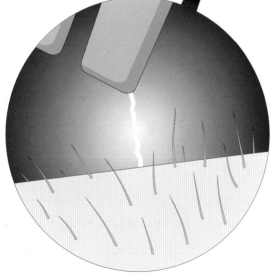

▲ ① **This diagram shows a spark moving between an arm and a comb. Notice also that hairs on the arm are standing on end – for an explanation of this see page 33.**

Sparks

A spark occurs when the electric charge that builds in one place is so great that it can flow through the air to reach an opposite charge somewhere else.

When you rub a comb on your clothes and then hold it close to your hand, you may see a tiny spark, just a few millimetres long (picture ①). Until the materials get very close, the charge on the comb cannot affect the charge on your hand.

Like charges attract. As there is now a negatively charged surface opposite a positively charged surface, charges can jump the gap. When this happens we see a spark.

In fact, we don't see the charge jump at all. What we actually see is the air 'catch fire' as the electricity flows through it!

Lightning

As we have seen, when two things brush together, they are likely to get charged. Water droplets in a thundercloud become charged when strong winds inside the cloud whisk them past one another at high speed.

A cloud gets many negatively charged droplets near its base. This

In this part of the cloud, water droplets carry a positive charge.

Lightning commonly travels from one region of a cloud to another. When the spark is hidden from view, people see the cloud lit up in layers. They call this sheet lightning.

The lower part of the cloud has a negative charge.

Some people call the bolts of lightning that travel between the ground and the cloud forked lightning.

The ground below the cloud is positively charged (even though the ground elsewhere is negatively charged).

▲ ② **This diagram shows a side view through a thundercloud. Notice the charges.**

produces positive charges in both the top of the cloud and on the ground below the cloud.

Because opposites attract, a spark can jump either between the bottom of the cloud and the ground or between the bottom of the cloud and the top of the cloud.

A flash of lightning is the world's biggest type of spark (picture ②). When a flash of lightning occurs, it passes through thousands of metres of air, so imagine what the charge must be for this to happen.

Thunder – the sound of sparks

A small spark makes a kind of crackling sound. This is the sound made as the air next to the spark is heated so fast that the air expands violently. This sends vibrations through the air in just the same way as when we bang a drum. This is how we hear a spark. Thunder is simply the sound of a massive spark, and the rumbling is the pattern of sounds made as the sound bounces off the layers of the cloud.

Weblink:www.CurriculumVisions.com/electricity

Magnets and magnetism

Magnetism is an invisible force that attracts and repels iron and steel.

A **MAGNET** is a piece of material that will attract pieces of iron or steel (picture ①). **MAGNETISM** is the invisible force that magnets produce. Anything that is attracted by a magnet is called a magnetic material.

▶ ① A permanent magnet will attract steel objects such as these paperclips. This magnet is called a horseshoe magnet because of its shape.

Patterns of magnetism

Magnets have some extraordinary properties. If you take two magnets and put them end to end, they may snap together (attract), or they may push apart (repel). To explain this, the magnets must have like and unlike ends. The ends of a magnet are usually called the south and north **POLES**. The effect is similar to static electricity (see page 32).

Magnets affect a wide area around them, not just the poles. This is called the **MAGNETIC FIELD**. You can see the magnetic field if you sprinkle some iron filings on a piece of card and then put a bar magnet (a straight magnet) under the card. The iron filings arrange themselves into a pattern of curving lines (picture ②). The lines pick out the (invisible) area of influence of the magnet (picture ③).

Permanent magnets

Some magnetic materials, such as steel, hold on to their magnetism. They are called permanent magnets. A bar magnet is a permanent magnet.

▶ ② You can see a pattern of magnetic attraction if you place a bar magnet under a piece of card or a sheet of paper. Get some fine iron powder (iron filings) and scatter this over the paper. Then tap the paper gently. The iron powder will make a pattern like the one shown here.

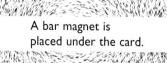

A bar magnet is placed under the card.

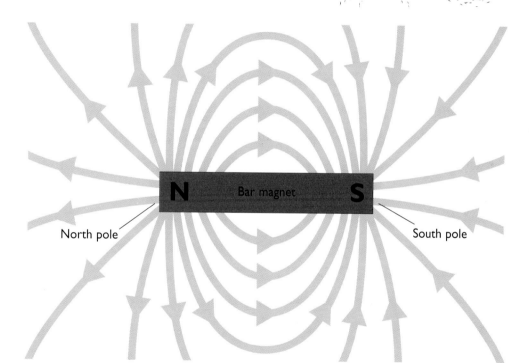

North pole   Bar magnet   South pole
N   S

◀ ③ Although you can't see it, this is what the magnetic pattern looks like. It is called the magnetic field. Notice the lines of magnetism go from the north to south pole of the magnet.

When other iron or steel objects are placed close to a permanent magnet, they will be attracted to it. In this way you can pick up, for example, a row of paperclips (picture ①). Because the paperclips are made of steel, when they are pulled away from the magnet, they will still hold together because they have now become magnets.

Uses of permanent magnets

Permanent magnets are important, but they have very limited uses. This is because they have one big disadvantage: you cannot control the magnetism of a permanent magnet. But you can make temporary controllable magnets using electricity, and when you do this, magnetism becomes extremely useful, as you will see on pages 38 to 41.

Electromagnets

An electromagnet is a magnet made by an electric current as it flows through a wire. It is the only controllable form of magnetism.

A wire acts like a bar magnet whenever electricity flows through it.

Magnetism produced by electricity is called **ELECTROMAGNETISM**. It is used in many devices, such as electric bells and electric motors. Most magnets we use today are **ELECTROMAGNETS**.

Although a single wire will produce some magnetism, the magnetism can be made much more powerful by making the wire into a coil (picture ①).

An electromagnet

The simplest form of electromagnet consists of 2 to 3 metres of insulated copper wire wound around a nail (picture ②).

When the ends of the wire are connected to a battery, it becomes a magnet and will attract iron or steel objects, such as small nails and paperclips.

A large version of this kind of electromagnet can be used on the end of a crane to move steel around in a factory or in a scrap yard.

▼ ① This diagram shows how an electromagnet works. As electricity flows through the coil of wire it produces a magnetic effect just as if there were an invisible bar magnet inside the coil (shown red in the diagram).

▼ ② The nail and coil of wire used to make an electromagnet.

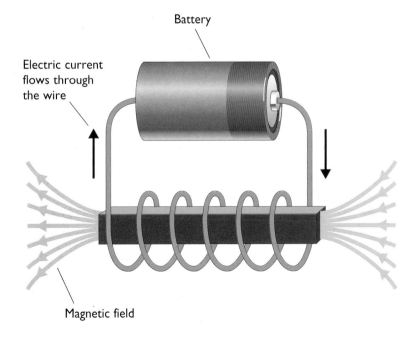

Battery

Electric current flows through the wire

Magnetic field

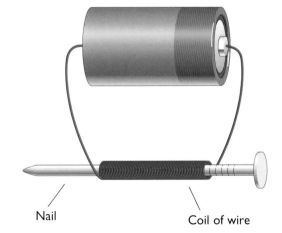

Nail

Coil of wire

A solenoid

An even more useful kind of electromagnet can be made if the wire is coiled around a tube instead of directly onto the nail (picture ③).

▼ ③ The nail and coil of wire used to make a solenoid.

If this coil is connected to a battery and a nail brought close to one end of the coil, the magnetism in the coil will draw the nail inside the coil and hold it there. A coil which causes movement in this way is called a solenoid.

An electric bell shows one use for a solenoid (picture ④).

▼ ④ This is a diagram of an electric bell. When electricity flows in the coil it turns the horseshoe-shaped piece of iron into a magnet. This attracts the iron strip that holds the hammer. The movement of the hammer against the bell makes it ring.

However, this movement also breaks the circuit and so the electromagnet is turned off. The springy metal can now return to rest, but as it does so, it completes the circuit again and so the electromagnet is turned back on. This process is repeated many times a second, giving a ringing sound.

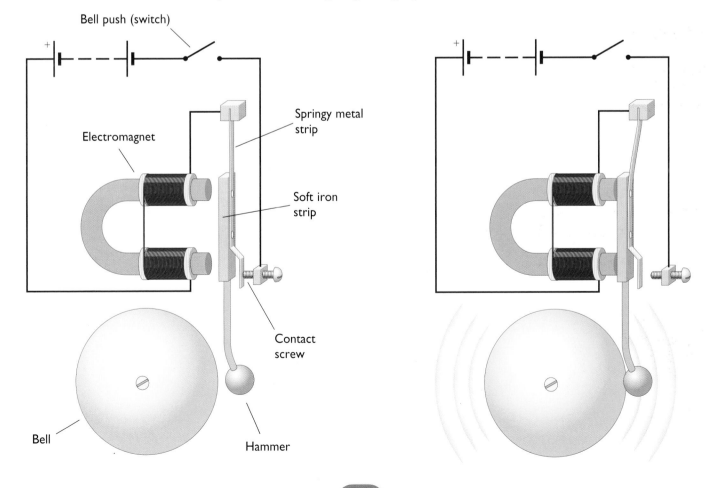

Bell push (switch)

Electromagnet

Springy metal strip

Soft iron strip

Contact screw

Bell

Hammer

Electric motors

One of the most useful ways of combining electricity and magnetism is to make a motor.

An electric motor is a device for changing electric power into turning movement.

How a motor works

The first electric motor ever made did not look like the kind of motor we see today. But every electric motor in the world has been developed from this first simple experiment. Picture ① shows you a version of this first motor.

A copper wire dangles in a metal dish containing salty water. In the centre of the dish is a magnet. When the copper wire and the dish are connected to the battery, something astonishing happens. The wire moves away from the magnet and then begins to rotate around it.

When the battery is connected, electricity flows through the wire, the salty water (salty water conducts electricity – see page 7) and the dish. The electric current flowing through the wire sets up a magnetic field around the wire. Because the wire is now magnetised, it is pushed away (repelled) by the magnet.

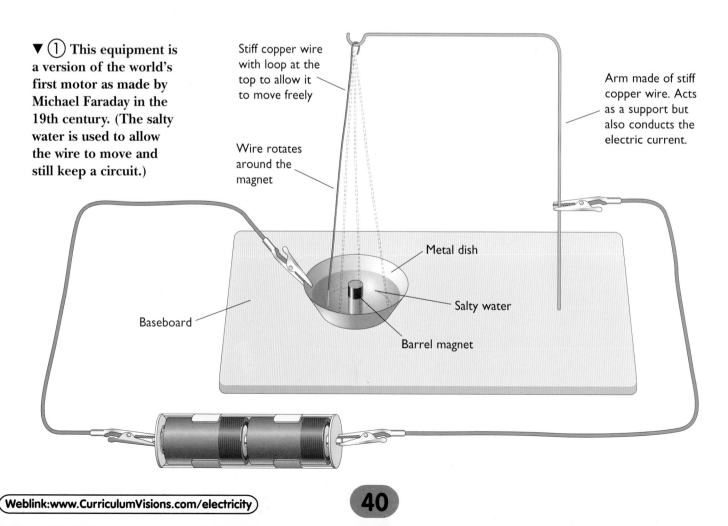

▼ ① **This equipment is a version of the world's first motor as made by Michael Faraday in the 19th century. (The salty water is used to allow the wire to move and still keep a circuit.)**

Stiff copper wire with loop at the top to allow it to move freely

Wire rotates around the magnet

Arm made of stiff copper wire. Acts as a support but also conducts the electric current.

Metal dish

Salty water

Barrel magnet

Baseboard

The wire goes round and round the magnet, trying to fall back to rest but, while the current flows, it never can. The round and round movement is a motor.

Modern motors

The modern electric motor is an inside-out version of the first motor made by Faraday (picture ②). The 'moving wire' is changed into a coil of wire and wrapped around the spindle of the motor.

The barrel magnet becomes a pair of curved magnets placed on each side of the coil.

The salty water of Faraday's experiment is changed into a pair of carbon rods that rest on a collar fixed to the drive shaft of the motor. The collar connects the power supply to the coil of wire.

Generators

A motor <u>uses</u> electricity, a **GENERATOR** <u>makes</u> electricity. Motors and generators are, therefore, the reverse of each other. A motor uses an electricity supply to turn the motor shaft, whereas in a generator the shaft is turned (for example by adding a water wheel to one end) and electricity flows out of the coil. This is how a power station generator works (see page 42).

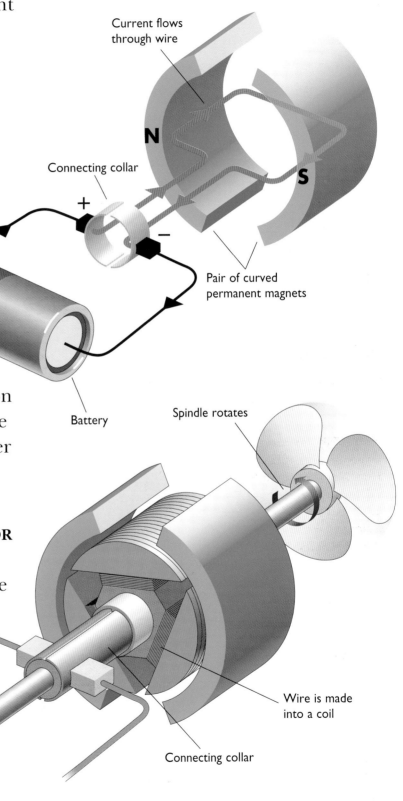

▼ ② A simple modern electric motor uses the same principles as Faraday's motor.

Current flows through wire

N

S

Connecting collar

+

−

Pair of curved permanent magnets

Battery

Spindle rotates

Wire is made into a coil

Connecting collar

Power supplies

Most of the things we do in the modern world depend on a power supply. This is how electricity gets from a power station to homes and factories.

The key to making electricity is a generator (see page 41). To generate electricity, the shaft of the generator has to be turned. The source of turning may be wind, running water or steam produced by burning coal. A building containing a generator is called a **POWER STATION** (picture ①).

Transmission lines

Once the electricity has been generated, it must be moved to where it is needed. In this book you have seen that electricity is moved by wires. We can choose to have a low voltage as a source of power, in which case we need to have a large current and, therefore, thick wires. Or, we can choose to use a high voltage. In this case we need a smaller current and can use thinner wires.

Thick wires are cumbersome, expensive and a lot of electricity leaks away from them. Electric power companies therefore use a high voltage.

Picture ① shows how power is taken from a power station to factories, offices and homes. The pattern of cables is called an **ELECTRICITY GRID**. You will see that the voltage in the cables (called **TRANSMISSION LINES**) from a power station is 400,000 volts. This is the most efficient voltage to carry electricity long distances. It is carried from the power station on high towers (**PYLONS**). Air is used as a cheap insulator (picture ②).

▼▶ ① The way electricity is carried from power stations to homes, offices and factories is called an electricity grid.

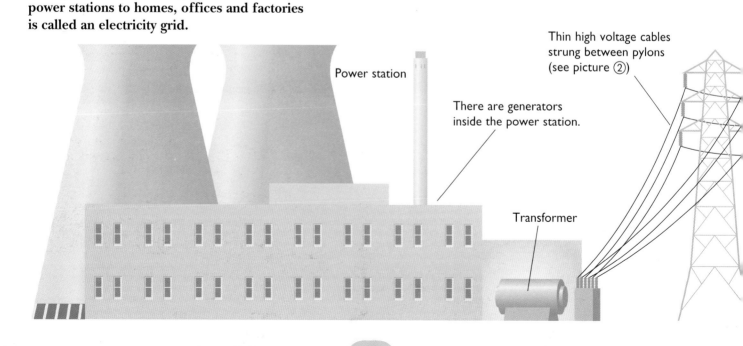

Power station

There are generators inside the power station.

Transformer

Thin high voltage cables strung between pylons (see picture ②)

▶ ② **A close-up of the overhead cable strung between pylons.**

This insulator is used to separate the cables from the metal of the pylon. It is made of a ceramic.

This is a conducting cable that carries electricity between pylons. It is made of a metal that is a good conductor, called aluminium. Notice how it consists of many wires twisted together.

Air is used as the insulator for this cable. As the cable hangs from a pylon high above the ground, it does not need a plastic coat.

When the electricity supply gets to the place where it is needed, the voltage is changed to about 240V using a piece of equipment called a **TRANSFORMER**. The cables leaving the transformer are usually insulated within plastic sheathing and buried underground (picture ③).

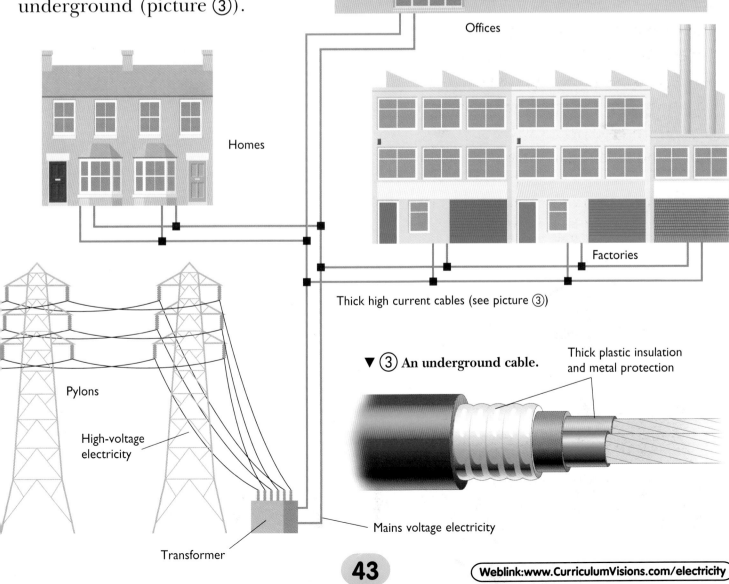

Offices

Homes

Factories

Thick high current cables (see picture ③)

Pylons

High-voltage electricity

▼ ③ **An underground cable.**

Thick plastic insulation and metal protection

Mains voltage electricity

Transformer

43

Electricity and the environment

Electricity seems a very clean form of energy. Here, we look to see how it is generated to find out if it really is so environmentally friendly.

Electricity seems like a very clean form of energy. There is no smoke pollution as with a wood fire, no **ACID RAIN** pollution as there might be with a coal fire, and no **GREENHOUSE WARMING** as there might be with a gas fire.

This is because electricity is a different form of energy to all the other kinds. Electricity is a secondary form of energy. Coal, gas and oil are all fuels – called **FOSSIL FUELS** – used to make electricity.

Look back at the power station diagram on page 42 and you will see

that the electricity is probably generated in a power station that burns coal, oil or gas as a fuel, or perhaps in one that burns rubbish collected from homes. So, although electricity itself is environmentally friendly, the way we generate it is not.

Another fuel that can be used to produce electricity is **NUCLEAR FUEL**. This does not produce pollution and so, from this point of view, it is better for the environment than fossil fuels. However, the risk of radiation leaking to the environment if a nuclear power station goes wrong has caused widespread concern.

▼ ① **These are the main ways in which electricity is generated.**

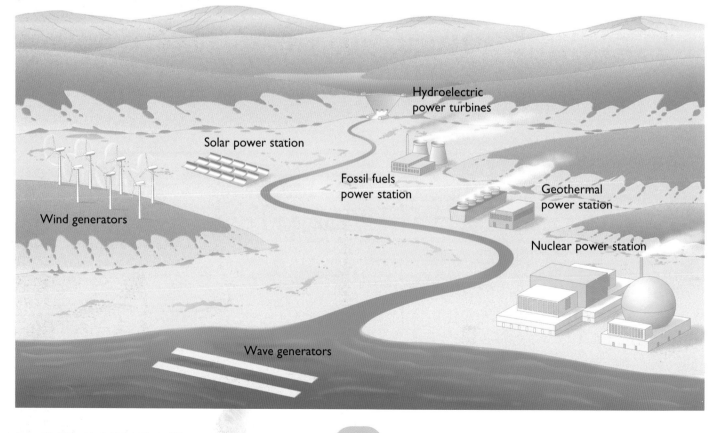

Hydroelectric power turbines

Solar power station

Fossil fuels power station

Geothermal power station

Wind generators

Nuclear power station

Wave generators

Green forms of electricity

It is possible to generate electricity without burning fuels at all or without having a radiation threat. These ways are:

- by using running water (called **HYDROELECTRIC POWER**, HEP);
- by using the sun (called **SOLAR POWER**);
- by using natural hot water (called **GEOTHERMAL POWER**); and
- by using the wind or the waves at sea.

Because no fuels are burned, no pollution is produced and so these are called 'green' forms of energy.

Of these three kinds of energy, HEP (picture ②) is by far the most important. But, to make it work, you have to have large, fast-flowing rivers, or reservoirs. These are not available everywhere.

It is only possible to use solar energy (picture ③) where the sun shines strongly for much of the year, and to use geothermal energy where natural hot springs occur.

It is only possible to use wind (picture ④) or wave generators in exposed places.

So, overall, green forms of energy cannot provide us with all of the electricity we need. The result is that we have to continue to rely on fossil fuels. This means we need to keep down the effect of burning fuels by using electricity more efficiently.

▼ ② HEP is generated by allowing water to flow through a turbine. It is the most important form of green energy.

▼ ③ Solar generators can be important, but only in places where the sun shines strongly.

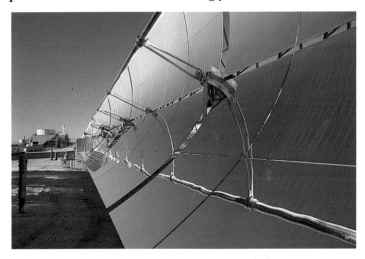

▼ ④ Wind generators mostly only yield small amounts of power or take up huge amounts of space, as you can see here. This is called a wind farm.

Glossary

ACID RAIN Rainfall that has become slightly acid because of pollution with gases released from (among other sources) power stations.

AMPS The short word for ampere, which is a measure of the electric current passing through a circuit. Can be written using the symbol 'A'.

APPLIANCE A device, or piece of equipment, that uses electricity. The name is used for complete pieces of electrical equipment, for example an iron or a washing machine.

BATTERY Any device that converts chemical energy into electrical energy. The word battery is properly used to mean a number of cells placed in line, but people tend to use the word more generally to mean any portable source of electricity, whether it is a single cell or many cells.

BUZZER A device for converting electricity into sound. It produces a relatively quiet buzzing sound.

CELL A device that generates electricity from a chemical reaction or from sunlight.
  The 'battery' we use in small devices, such as a torch, is a single electric cell and is correctly called a 'dry cell'. Dry cells contain a damp paste of chemicals that produce electricity.
  A car battery, in contrast, is made up of lots of cells and uses liquid chemicals.
  A solar cell is very different as it converts sunlight into electricity.

CHARGE The build-up of electricity on the surface of an insulator. People use the word, for example, when talking about static electricity. There can be a positive charge or a negative charge.

CIRCUIT, ELECTRIC CIRCUIT A path that links a source of electricity, such as a battery or mains electricity, to devices that use electricity, such as a light bulb or buzzer.

CIRCUIT DIAGRAM A simple line drawing that shows the components of a circuit and how they are connected.

CIRCUIT TESTER A device that allows you to investigate what is happening inside a circuit. Circuit testers often have a needle that swings to indicate current, voltage or resistance. However, circuit testers may have a digital display instead of a needle. A circuit tester can also be called a meter or multimeter.

COMPASS A small steel needle that can spin on a pivot and point the direction of a magnetic source.

COMPONENT A device in a circuit that uses or controls electricity. A buzzer, a light bulb or similar devices are components. Batteries and wires are not components.

CONTACTS Part of a device designed to make a good connection to a circuit so that electricity can flow through the device.
  Contacts come in many forms. They may be flat metal blades in a switch, or pins of a plug, or the curved base of a light bulb.

CURRENT, ELECTRIC CURRENT The flow of electricity through a circuit. Electric current is measured in Amps (A).

DRY CELL A cell or battery that contains chemicals that are not liquid. Instead dry cells contain a chemical paste. Dry cells are the 'batteries' we use in small devices, such as a torch.

EARTH WIRE A wire connected to the metal parts of some appliances, such as cookers and heaters, to provide a safe route for electricity to flow in the event of a live wire accidentally touching the metal.

ELECTRIC MOTOR A device that converts electricity into a turning movement. Most motors have a spindle, which is connected to machines to make them work.

ELECTRICAL CONDUCTOR Any material that allows electricity to easily flow through it. Metals are the most common conductors used for electric circuits (e.g. wires).

ELECTRICAL INSULATOR Any material that does not allow electricity to flow through it easily. Plastic is commonly used as an insulator for electric circuits (e.g. plug cases and the sleeves around wires).

ELECTRICITY A form of energy. Electricity can either flow through materials as a current (current electricity) or remain static on the surface of materials (static electricity).

ELECTRICITY GRID A network of cables designed to connect power stations with their customers in offices, homes, schools and factories. The cables are often carried on tall overhead pylons across country, but buried underground in cities.

ELECTROMAGNET A magnet produced by an electric current flowing through a coiled wire.

ELECTROMAGNETISM Magnetism produced by electricity.

ENERGY The ability to do work or make something change. Electrical energy is the amount of electrical power produced per second.

FILAMENT The tightly coiled wire inside an electric light bulb. Electricity is passed through the filament to produce light. A filament is made of a metal with a high resistance and a high melting point.

FORCE An influence that can cause something to move (e.g. the magnetic force surrounding a magnet can make iron filings move).

FOSSIL FUELS Fuels that have been formed in the past by natural processes. The main fossil fuels are coal, oil and natural gas.

FUSE A piece of fine wire made of a metal with a low melting point. A fuse is designed to melt if the amount of current flowing in a circuit becomes dangerously large.

GENERATOR A machine for producing electricity. It is like a motor in reverse, where the spindle is turned and electricity flows from the surrounding coiled wire.

GEOTHERMAL POWER Power produced by the natural steam found near some volcanoes.

GREENHOUSE WARMING The extra warming of the Earth's atmosphere as a result of carbon dioxide gas being released into the air. One of the main sources of carbon dioxide is fossil fuels which are burned to generate electricity. Also called the 'Greenhouse Effect'.

HYDROELECTRIC POWER Power produced by turning a generator using fast-flowing water. Hydroelectric power stations are located near dams, or on large rivers.

LIGHT BULB A glass bulb filled with gas and containing a filament. When electricity flows through the filament it glows white hot and gives out light.

LIGHTNING A natural spark produced between charged layers of cloud, or between a cloud and the ground.

LIVE WIRE The wire connected to the positive side of the mains electricity supply.

MAGNET A piece of iron, steel or other material that will attract another piece of iron or steel. Something is said to be magnetic if it acts like a magnet.

MAGNETIC FIELD The region around a magnet in which magnetic forces can be detected.

MAGNETISM The force that attracts and repels iron and some other materials.

MAINS ELECTRICITY The electricity supply that is delivered to homes, schools, offices and factories. It is normally 240V.

NEGATIVE TERMINAL The negative end of a battery.

NEUTRAL WIRE The mains electricity wire connected to the negative side of the electricity supply.

NUCLEAR FUEL A material used in a nuclear power station to produce electrical energy.

OHMS A measure of the resistance of a component in a circuit. Can be written using the symbol 'Ω'.

PARALLEL CIRCUIT An electrical circuit in which the components are connected side by side (in parallel) to the battery so they all get the same voltage.

POLE The attracting or repelling end of a magnet. Magnets have north and south poles.

POSITIVE TERMINAL The positive end of a battery.

POWER Electric power is the amount of electricity needed to do something in a certain time. Power is measured in watts. Watts can be written with the symbol W.
Power is more generally used to mean a supply of energy, such as electrical energy (e.g. power station).

POWER STATION A place where electricity is generated, most usually by burning coal, oil or gas, to turn water into steam, and then using high pressure steam to turn the shaft of the generator.

PYLONS Metal towers that can support electricity cables safely across countryside.

RESISTANCE Part of an electric circuit that opposes the flow of electric current, and so turns electric energy into heat. Resistance is measured in ohms.

SERIES CIRCUIT An electrical circuit in which the battery and all the components are connected end to end in a single loop.

SHORT CIRCUIT A situation where, for example, the positive and negative ends of a battery or mains supply are connected directly together, causing a large current to flow. Fuses are designed to melt when short circuits occur.

SOLAR POWER The electrical power produced from the sun's rays.

SPARK The sudden flow of electricity between two charged surfaces.

STATIC ELECTRICITY A form of electricity that builds up on the surfaces of insulating materials. It consists of positive and negative charges.

SWITCH A device for breaking the flow of electricity in a circuit.

TRANSFORMER A device for changing the voltage of an electricity supply. It is mainly used to step down the very high voltage carried by transmission lines to the lower (240V) voltage needed for home use.

TRANSMISSION LINES Large cables designed to carry very high voltage electricity from the power station to where it is needed.

VOLTAGE The electrical 'pressure' that a battery or other source of electricity can provide. It is measured in volts. A single dry battery normally provides 1.5 volts; a mains supply provides 240 volts. Volts can be written using by the symbol 'V'.

Index